Introduction

This booklet contains 12 generic lesson plans for Big Writing that may be used

1. Consecutively to 'get a novice going' and give confidence.
2. As a full year's teaching programme for Big Writing.

> Use '**Next Time...**' notes at the end of each lesson plan to adapt for reuse

3. To complement work across the wider curriculum, through the adaption of lessons, as noted at the end of many plans.
4. As occasional lessons in a programme of school-planned Big Writing that works to the school's literacy programme and / or 'Creative Curriculum'.

Every lesson plan shares the same objectives:

> **Objective 1:** To widen children's vocabulary.
> **Objective 2:** To raise standards in writing.

1. Loop Games Lesson

Objective 1: To widen children's vocabulary.
Objective 2: To raise standards in writing.

Requirements:
Each child will have:
3 blank cards numbered 1, 2, 3.
A card from a 'WOW' word Loop Game
(Less able may need to work in a pair sharing a card. More able may have 2 cards).
Individual whiteboards and felt tips.
Blank white paper (optional).

Start Lesson Here

A. Chant (with hand action) "What have we got to remember? The V.C.O.P" or sing the V.C.O.P. song to the tune of Y.M.C.A.

B. Play a 'WOW' Word Loop Game (Available from Andrell Education Limited OR use the Glossary on the 'Big Word Games' disc to make your own).

C. Target child (chosen by the teacher) reads her/ his word again (E.g. 'apparition').

D. Groups/ pairs discuss the word and agree a meaning.

E. 'Call My Bluff' (Appendix 2) with the word (E.g. apparition) & 3 numbered meanings (Should be meanings of other words in the Loop Game so they look / sound familiar.)

F. Groups/ pairs hold up number (1, 2 or 3) for the one they think is right.

G. Blank screen / number cards restacked in the middle of the tables / teacher says the word (E.g. apparition) / class spell out. (Or teacher chooses a target child to spell out) while 'writing' with bare finger on table top.

H. Groups / pairs think up 2 / 3 / 4 synonyms for target word (E.g. apparition = ghost, vision, spectre).

I. Numbered words fading in and out or spinning on the whiteboard, including synonyms & antonyms and some words unrelated to the target word.

J. Groups / pairs 'grab' numbers for true synonyms & write (large) with fat felt tip pens on paper or on whiteboards.

K. "Show me" / answers come on the screen, both the number and the word.

L. Feedback of any synonyms thought of by the groups / pairs not showing on the screen (From H).

M. Repeat items 7 to 11 with antonyms. (Use or do not use to adjust the timings).

N. Give a focus related to current learning in other lessons / things known to the children (Should be a suitable context for use of the target word eg apparition could relate to a poem or story read, a field trip to an old house, a popular cartoon or movie etcetera). Groups / pairs make up sentences with the target word in.

O. Feedback.

P. Change focus to other learning or situations (Should be suitable context for use of the target word) plus a suitable 'Power Opener' (See Appendix 2), groups / pairs make up a new sentence with the

4

Power Opener & the target word. (Or children could choose own Power Opener).

Q. Class spell the word while writing with bare finger on their own other arm. (A textured surface. Fine sand paper is also very good for this).

R. The target word appears on the screen.

> **Next Time...** this whole session may be repeated once a month, targeting a different word from the Loop Game = 40 lessons.

2. Spot The Difference Lesson

Objective 1: To widen children's vocabulary.
Objective 2: To raise standards in writing.

Requirements:
Each child will have:
Number cards 1, 2, and 3.
Individual whiteboards and felt tips.
Blank white paper (Optional)

Passage 1:
Once upon a time there was a little girl called Red Riding Hood. One day her mother asked her to take some cake to her Grandma. Grandma lived in a cottage in the wood. Red Riding Hood loved the wood. She liked the flowers and she liked to hear the birds singing in the trees. The woodcutter was working in the woods. He asked Red Riding Hood where she was going. She told him she was taking cake to her grandmother. He told her to be careful. He had just seen a wolf in the wood.

Passage 2:
Red Riding Hood, who was a vivacious little girl, lived on the periphery of the wood with her mother. One glorious, warm morning her mother asked her to visit her grandmother (who lived in a charming cottage in the heart of the wood) taking her a cake for her supper. Red Riding Hood adored being in the wood. She particularly enjoyed admiring the abundant flowers and enjoying the sweet songs of the birds in the foliage. On that particular day the woodcutter was busy trimming some of the bushes and he greeted her cheerfully, asking her where she was going. The young girl explained that she was bearing cake to her elderly grandmother. "Proceed very carefully," the woodcutter cautioned her. "A huge fox just passed this way. Be vigilant."

   **Start Lesson Here**

A. Chant (with hand action) "What have we got to remember? The V.C.O.P." or sing the V.C.O.P. song to the tune of Y.M.C.A.

B. Call My Bluff (See Appendix 2): 'vivacious'
    1. Adventurous and happy to take risk   2. Lively and bubbly   3. Beautiful (all on screen).

C. Groups / pairs discuss / choose number card 1, 2, or 3. Find the card with the chosen number.

D. "Show me".

E. Spell the word (still on screen) while writing with a bare finger on the table top or fine sand paper.

F. Spell the word while writing up in the air to the left with a pen / pencil.

G. Close eyes and spell the word while writing on other arm with bare finger.

H. Put up the two paragraphs (Page 7) on the whiteboard. They may both be shortened by cutting off after the words 'trees' (Passage 1) and 'foliage' (Passage 2) if the teacher feels they are too long. Read together if needed, then read in small groups, and then read together again until all children can read both, at least by 'sight reading'.

I. 'Guesstimate' the levels. (First is a Level 3 and second is a low L 5).

J. Spell 'vivacious' twice from the screen.
K. Close eyes and spell 'vivacious' while drawing letters on table top or fine sand paper with a bare fingertip.
L. Groups / pairs discuss the word 'periphery'. Agree what they think it means.
M. Call My Bluff: 'periphery'   1. On the edge / at the boundary   2. Route or journey   3. Estate or mansion that owns the wood. (All on the board)
N. Groups / pairs discuss / choose number card 1, 2, or 3 as the card with the correct number.
O. "Show me". Had they found right meaning in Step L?
P. Groups / pairs list 'WOW' words in passage 2 on their whiteboards. Guess the meanings.
Q. Which 'WOW' word would you steal and why?
R. 'WOW' words circling or fading in and out on the whiteboard screen. Did you find them all? Vivacious, periphery, glorious, charming, adored, particularly, abundant, proceed, vigilant.
S. Line up these words on the left, meanings on the right in the wrong order on the whiteboard or on a handout between 2 or 3. Match correctly by joining with a line.
T. Target one or more for 'Make me up a sentence about…' (relevant to the story in the passages).
U. Groups / pairs find places for one Power Opener in Passage 2 (see Appendix 2). Discuss the possibilities.
V. Groups / pairs find places for use of all 3 pieces of Power Punctuation = ? ! … in Passage 2.
W. Teacher shows Passage 2 pre-prepared earlier, to show potential answers (below).
X. Class read new Passage 2 together.
Y. Blank screen, repeat steps DEF with 'vivacious'.

Cool Down

A. Dramatic picture on screen ('Interesting Pictures' download, please see Appendix 3) groups / pairs think up 3 or more 'ing' words for what's happening. Make up a sentence about the picture that opens with one of the 'ing' words.

Additional Optional Activity:
Role play or recount (or both) the full story of Red Riding Hood.

Model passage 2, edited.
Red Riding Hood, who was a vivacious little girl, lived on the periphery of the wood with her mother. One glorious, sunny morning her mother asked her to visit her grandmother (who lived in a charming cottage in the heart of the wood) taking her cake for her supper. Red Riding Hood adored being in the wood! She particularly enjoyed admiring the abundant flowers and enjoying the sweet songs of the birds in the foliage. On that particular day the woodcutter was busy trimming some of the bushes and he greeted her cheerfully. "Where are you going? He asked. Explaining that she was bearing cake to her elderly grandmother, the young girl replied to his question. "Proceed very carefully," the woodcutter cautioned her. "A huge dog fox just passed this way. Be vigilant…"

Next Time… use the differentiated texts in the Appendices to change the 2 texts and repeat the lesson once a half term = 10 lessons.

3. Sea Monsters Lesson

Objective 1: To widen children's vocabulary.
Objective 2: To raise standards in writing.

Requirements:
4 blank cards & thick felt tips on each table, dictionaries.
Picture on the white board or hard copy between 2 or 3.

Each child will have:
A whiteboard and felt tips.

Available in the 'Interesting Pictures' download. Please see Appendix 3.

 **Start Lesson Here**

A. Pairs: Are they scary? Are they beautiful? Talk about it. Choose 3 'WOW' describing words for them.

B. Write one of the 3 'WOW' words on each of the 3 Cards. Check the spelling in dictionaries.

C. Move round and meet one other pair. Take it in turns to ask each other to spell each of the 3 'WOW' words and give a definition. Pairs may discuss before answering.

D. Pairs each steal a word they particularly like from the other pair and give one of their own in exchange.

E. Move on to other pairs and repeat.

F. Back in seats; make up sentences with the 'WOW' words in, about the sea creatures.

G. Feedback.

H. Teacher puts up 3 of her/his own 'WOW' words: e.g. any of 3 of exotic / fearsome / sinister / gruesome / grotesque / fascinating / sumptuous / baffling. Children make up sentences.

I. Teacher puts up 3 of her/his own sentences OR scribes 3 from children. E.g. 1. 'The exotic sea monster hovered amongst the weeds.' 2. 'The fearsome sea monster lurked in the deep.' 3. 'The sinister sea monster watched and waited...'

J. Pairs discuss new 'WOW' words (hovered / lurked) and agree meaning. Write the suggested meaning on whiteboards.

K. Show me. Teacher puts the correct definition on the whiteboard.

L. Pairs to find 'ly' Power Openers (see Appendix 2) they could put on the front of each of the 3 sentences, against the clock (could be just teacher counting back from 10 to 0, must have done all 3).

M. Teacher takes feedback and then either scribes some of children's or puts up models on the whiteboard. E.g. 1. Patiently, the exotic... 2. Menacingly, the fearsome... 3. Hungrily... (More examples: Sinisterly...Silently...Watchfully...Threateningly...Formidably...)

N. Give pupils the following passage on the board. Children to up-level as a class.
   a. 'The sea monster was waiting for something it could eat, to pass by. It looked threatening because it was so different from anything the divers had seen before. They were afraid to approach.'

O. Teacher inserts some of the suggestions to up-level e.g. 'Menacingly, the sea monster lurked, hungrily, in the dimness of the deep. He was awaiting his prey, which would inevitably stray into his path. As the divers had never seen this strange apparition before, it felt threatening. Hence, they were reluctant to approach!'

P. Put both paragraphs together on board and play 'Spot The Difference'.

Cool Down

A. Are there any words the children don't know the meaning of?

B. Call My Bluff (see Appendix 2): Give 3 new 'WOW' words relevant to the theme on the whiteboard. Children have 10 seconds to choose correct definitions.

C. Correct ones spin on the white board.

Next Time... change the picture and repeat the lesson once a half term = infinite lessons. Google 'Interesting Pictures' or download the bank of 'interesting pictures' from our website (see Appendix 3).

4. Victor Von Cleef Lesson

Objective 1: To widen children's vocabulary.
Objective 2: To raise standards in writing.

Requirements:
'VCOP Games' disc for Victor Von Cleef game as a warm up OR find a cartoon picture of a thief on the web.

Start Lesson Here

A. Picture of Victor on the screen. In pairs: What could he be about to steal from school? (Not to do with Big Writing). TV? PC? Safe?

B. Children creep round room like a thief. Teacher makes loud bang, thieves freeze. Repeat. Think of 'WOW' words for how they are moving. E.g. creeping, stealing (unpick the different meanings), tiptoeing, sneaking.

C. Share. Teacher scribes on the whiteboard.

D. Groups / pairs discuss and agree 3 'ly' words for how he approaches.

E. Feedback.

F. Show a range of words on screen: e.g. stealthily / cautiously / surreptitiously / quietly / silently / ominously / tentatively / furtively

G. Pairs discuss each word and agree how each is different from other. Which are synonyms? (1st & 3rd are, 4th & 5th are. Last one goes with the 1 and 3.)

H. Pairs choose one word and use in a sentence about Victor. E.g. 'Victor Von Cleef crept stealthily into the school.'

I. Feedback.

J. Give the sentence a Power Opener (see Appendix 2) if they didn't first time e.g. 'Stealthily, Victor Von Cleef crept into the school.'

K. Make up a second sentence that uses Power Punctuation (see Appendix 2). Feedback. E.g. "He heard a noise... what was that sound?' OR 'CRASH!'

L. Choose one of the things he is going to steal. Pairs discuss and choose 3 'WOW' describing words. Write on white boards. E.g. incredible, invaluable, valuable, expensive, sophisticated, 'state-of the-art', ultrasonic, astounding, amazing...

M. "Show me". Show the range in 'L' on the whiteboard and add any from the class.

N. Make up a sentence about what he intended to steal. E.g. 'He was intending to steal the incredible, new PC from the office.' OR 'He was intending to steal the invaluable contents of the sophisticated school safe.'

O. Three sentences are now on the whiteboard from J, K, and N. All read. E.g. **'Stealthily Victor Von Cleef crept into the school. He heard a noise... what WAS that sound? He was intending to steal the incredible, new PC from the office.'**

P. Should the sentences be reordered? Discussion: Could we improve the order? E.g. 'Stealthily Victor Von Cleef crept into the school. He was intending to steal the incredible new PC from the office. He heard a noise... what WAS that sound?'

Q. What level would a piece written like this be? Pairs make up one more sentence that must include a second, different Power Opener (see Appendix 2) and a second, different piece of Power Punctuation (see Appendix 2). Feedback. Teacher scribes the additional one or puts up the paragraph done in 'P'. E.g. 'Cautiously, Victor crept forward...'

R. Children read the new paragraph. Give final, new sentences added on to the paragraph, e.g. 'BOOM! Victor froze as a _____ explosion rocked the foundations of the building.' Pairs discuss & select a WOW describing word for the explosion. Write on their whiteboards.

S. Show me. Examples on board E.g. massive / enormous / deafening / earth shattering / sonic etc.

Cool Down

A. Snappy Synonyms: Count backwards from 10 to 0 for each word, pairs to make 3 or more synonyms e.g. mute / evil / secure (**mute = silent, noiseless, quiet; evil = wicked, bad, devilish; secure = safe, protected, locked**).

Additional Optional Activity:
Use VCOP Games disc to play 'Victor Von Cleef, Punctuation Thief'.

Next Time...change the stimulus character (Super Heroes? Notorious cartoon villains?) and repeat the lesson = infinite lessons.

	5. Dinosaur Dialogue Lesson

Objective 1: To widen children's vocabulary.
Objective 2: To raise standards in writing.

Requirements:
A3 paper and Blu-Tack.

Each child will have:
A small whiteboard and a thick felt tip pen.

Excerpt from 'Little PALS for Big Text: Dialogue' by Ros Wilson

Setting:	The wood.
Hannah	**Come on you two. We need to hurry or we will be late for tea.**
Max	I am tired. Slow down Hannah.
Hannah	**We cannot slow down Max. Mum will be cross if we are late.**
Farrah	I am tired too. Shall we sit down for a while?
Hannah	**Well, just two minutes then. Here, sit on this log.**
Max	What is that moving in the bushes?
Farrah	**Oh gosh!**
Hannah	It can't be – it looks like a little dinosaur!
Max	**Oh, how sweet. It would be great to have that as a pet!**

 **Start Lesson Here**

- **A.** In groups of 3, read the dialogue together. Allocate parts and 'act' script. Discuss importance of expression and use of the voice. Reread.
- **B.** Choose 2 groups to 'perform'.
- **C.** Ask the class where there is a contraction (can't). What is it short for? How do we contract words? Why?
- **D.** Pairs / groups = 3 places where words could be CONTRACTED or shortened by taking out letters and using an apostrophe (talk only).
  1. (Hannah 1 = we'll 2. Max 1 = I'm 3. Hannah 2 = can't / Mum'll / we're 4. Farrah 1 = I'm 5. Max 2 = What's).
- **E.** In pairs, record 3 expanded forms and their contractions on small whiteboards, from the dialogue.
- **F.** "Show me".

G. Range of contractions whizz round or fade in and out on screen. Children shout the full form. Eg can't / won't / hasn't / isn't / doesn't / mustn't / let's / I'm. Children shout 'can not' / 'will not' / 'has not' etcetera.

H. Reverse = expanded form fading in and out. Shout the contractions. Eg I have / We are / They are / They have / I would / She would / It is / There is / We would / We have / Does not.

I. Pairs / groups = find two places for a Power Opener (see Appendix 2). Record on whiteboard. Show me. Take some examples to see how used. Eg 'Unfortunately, we can't slow down Max.' 'Having it as a pet…'

J. How many pieces of Power Punctuation are there? (2 = ? and !) Which is missing? Where could you work in ellipses? Eg to replace any one of the full stops in the first 5 lines of speech. Remember to take out the capital letter as well.

K. Is there a 'WOW' word? (No, unless this was written by a six year old). Where could you insert one? Pairs discuss. Choose one & say where it would go. Discuss as a group / model examples. Record in pairs.

L. Show me. Choose 3 to model. Eg 'irate' instead of cross / 'weary' instead of the second tired / 'lurking' instead of moving / 'adorable' instead of sweet / 'minute' instead of little etcetera.

M. How many adjectives are there (describing words for nouns or things)? (Answer = 1 = little). Pairs: Where else could you put one? Find as many places as you can. Share as a group. List on A3 paper with thick markers. Blu Tack on windows. Eg describe the log / the bushes / second adjective for the dinosaur / the pet. Which are 'WOW's? Can we think of more?

N. How many adverbs (describing verbs or 'doing' words) can pairs think up? Share as a group. Record on A3 with felt tips and Blu Tack below the adjectives. How many are WOWs? Can we think of more?

O. Pairs: make up Power Sentences about the dinosaur (2 out of the 3 Power features = Power Opener / Power Punctuation / 'WOW' words). Share in groups. Group choose the one they like best for feedback.

Cool Down

A. Call My Bluff:

Perambulate:

1. To delay or make someone late
2. To eat rapidly
3. To walk…

Answer = 3. Use the word in a sentence linked to a bit of the dialogue
eg. The children liked to perambulate in the dense wood.

Next Time… use texts from the range of 'Little PALS for Big Texts' to repeat the lesson = 10 lessons.

6. Alliteration Poem Lesson

Objective 1: To widen children's vocabulary.
Objective 2: To raise standards in writing.

Requirements:
A copy or copies of the poem below.
A3 paper, Blu-Tack and felt tips.

From 'The Little Book of Big Poems' by Ros Wilson.

Sensational Alliterative Sentences

Stupendous, sensational sentences,
Serendipitous words in a string!
Sweet stanzas styled with hissing sound
Shape verses simply stunning.
So select an assorted sample
Of 's' words, just don't stop,
And script your poetic celebration
So sentimental, you won't swop!

(The poem above may be on the white board or the flip chart or on paper between twos).

 **Start Lesson Here**

- **A.** In pairs/ 3s, count how many 'WOW' words they can find.
- **B.** Go through the poem and work out how to say each of the 'WOW' words. (Stupendous, sensational, serendipitous, stanzas, stunning, select, assorted, script, sentimental).
- **C.** Read the poem as a class, twice.
- **D.** Pairs: count the's's in the poem (39 – remember to include the title).
- **E.** Take each of the 'WOW' words in turn.(eg stupendous / sensational / serendipity / stanzas) Children discuss in 2s. Do they know the meaning? Join into groups, do they know the meanings? Use dictionaries to find the words. Could do it as a Dictionary Game (see Appendix 2): race against a countdown of 10 to 1 (or a timer) to find each word.
- **F.** Pairs: How many meanings do you know for 'script'? What does it mean in this context? Discuss as a group.
- **G.** Feedback and discuss.
- **H.** How many 's' describing words (adjectives) can pairs list on whiteboards, related to each of the following in turn: the beach / school / birthdays.
- **I.** Groups, on A3 paper with felt tips: How many 'ly' Power Openers can they think of starting with 's' ? Blu Tack on windows. Read all others. Steal a favourite. (Slowly... Stealthily... Softly... Sweetly... Sensitively... etcetera.
- **J.** Pairs on paper, make up two sentences with strings of 's' words about any one of the three stimuli in H. Use two of the 's' Power Openers from any sheets. Read out some. Eg 'Softly shining on the silver sand,

the summer sun shone steadily.' 'Slowly, sad children staggered fearfully towards their savage teachers in school.' 'Sweetly smiling siblings proffer sparkling parcels of sensational gifts for their special birthdays.'

- **K.** Pairs on whiteboard: List as many words as you can that rhyme or nearly rhyme with 'sun'. Eg sun / fun / ton / one / bun / run / done / begun / even / gun / glum / pun / won.
- **L.** In pairs, use rhyming words to make up poems about one of the three stimuli in H. Include at least one example of alliteration. Scribe neatly on A3 with felt tips. Blu Tack on windows (teacher has taken down the earlier lists). Move along windows reading the poems. Praise each other.

E.g.

**We all love
Holiday fun,
Playing on soft sands
In the sparkling sun.
Swimming in the sea
Then rest, then run,
And staggering slowly home
When the day is done.**

Or

**Birthday fun,
Presents by the ton,
Party games won
And cake for everyone.**

Next Time… Use another poem from 'The Little Book of Big Poems' to plan another lesson = 40 lessons.

7. Wave Lesson

Objective 1: To widen children's vocabulary.
Objective 2: To raise standards in writing.

Requirements:
A copy of the picture below on the whiteboard or hard copy between 2s / 3s.
A3 paper and felt tips.
Personal whiteboards.

Available in the 'Interesting Pictures' download. Please see Appendix 3.

   **Start Lesson Here**

A. Pairs on whiteboards: How many 'WOW' words can you find to describe this wave? "Show me". Each person chooses a favourite as own target word. Eg mighty... enormous...powerful... powering... towering... gigantic... threatening...surging.... etcetera.

B. Teacher chooses a word or chooses a child to give his/her word. Race to find the word in the thesaurus against count from 10 to 1. All read synonyms out. Do you want to trade or keep?

C. Give each of the following 3 'Power Openers' on the white board. in turn, children make up sentences about the wave using each of the Power Openers AND their personal target 'WOW' describing word: Surging / Cascading / Powering (do class need to discuss the meaning of any of these openers first?)

D. Children make up their own sentences with one of the 'Power Openers' and an additional WOW word from A. Eg Surging towards the beach, the tremendous wave threatened the village.

E. What might have caused this wave? Discuss. Eg Hurricane / Tsunami / Water Spout (like a tornado but over the sea) Earthquake / Cliff

16

F. Pairs, choose the cause they like best.

G. Give each of the following openers in turn. In pairs, make up 3 new sentences about the formation of this wave, starting with each of the following 'ly' openers: Angrily / Powerfully / Dramatically. Pairs scribe on A3 or white boards. E.g. Powerfully towering above the land, the wave was driven landward by the hurricane.

H. Pairs: on whiteboards, how many 'WOW' describing words (adjectives) can you think of that could go into your sentence? Choose one and insert it. Each one of the pair read the new sentence followed by their personal sentence from D. Praise each other.
E.g. 'Surging towards the beach, the tremendous wave threatened the village. Powerfully towering above the land, the wave was driven landward by the hurricane.'

I. How might you feel if you were in the sea and got caught up in this wave? Group discussion.

J. Children stand and model motion / movements they might experience.

K. In pairs /threes, list as many 'WOW' describing words for feelings on A3 with felt tips. Blu-Tack onto windows. Move along and read all lists. Choose any two words you would like to steal. E.g. terrified / exhausted / petrified / horrified.

L. Children make up a new sentence as though caught inside the wave using their chosen words. This one should NOT have a 'Power Opener'. (Discuss 'purple prose' or over use of 'Power Features': see Appendix 2)
E.g. 'I was petrified as the great wave swept me up and buffeted me about.'

M. Each read their 3 sentences in turn and praise each other.
E.g. 'Surging towards the beach, the tremendous wave threatened the village. Powerfully towering above the land, the wave was driven landward by the hurricane. I was petrified as the great wave swept me up and buffeted me about.'

Cool Down

A. Call My Bluff: Turbulent = 1. Very fast 2. In violent commotion 3. Rounded or circular. Children choose. Teacher gives the answer (= 2)

B. Children race to find synonyms for turbulent in the dictionary against count from 10 back to 1.

Next Time…repeat the lesson using another interesting picture = infinite lessons.

8. Super Heroes Lesson

Objective 1: To widen children's vocabulary.
Objective 2: To raise standards in writing.

Requirements:
A3 paper and felt tips.
Personal whiteboards.

A. Call My Bluff (See Appendix 2): Decimate: 1. To do calculations 2. To chop up 3. To destroy. Pairs discuss and agree. Group discusses.

B. Dictionary Race to count back from 10 to 0 to check meaning of 'decimate'.

C. Group brainstorm; natural events that could cause the decimation of this school. Eg Earthquakes / hurricanes / tornados / Tsunami / gas explosion?

D. Make up a sentence with an 'ing' Power Opener and the word 'decimate' or 'decimated' in, about this school. Share with friend. Share as a group. Praise each other. Eg Crumbling to the ground, the school was decimated by the force of the hurricane.

E. Pairs: Create an oral Super Hero. Give him/ her a name and a description. Share as a group. Children stand and move round room like Super Heroes.

F. Make up a Power Sentence about the Super Hero coming to the rescue of those trapped in the school. Share with a friend. Share as a group.
E.g. Swooping swiftly through the stratosphere, the Super Hero zoomed to our rescue. (The alliteration was not asked for, but may be remembered from Lesson 6.)

G. How many real words can children make out of the word 'decimation'? Record on white boards.

H. Show me. Who has most? Any challenges? Use dictionaries if so. Eg dice, dime, date, dame, dine, mate, mite, mine etcetera.

I. Thesaurus Race to find synonyms for decimate while teacher counts back from 10 to 0.

J. Groups brainstorm 'WOW' describing words for the destruction of the school. Eg devastating / shattering / distressing / totally / utterly / tragically.

K. Children make up a word picture of the school when it has been decimated. Use 'WOW' adjectives. Eg The school was totally devastated and lay, strewn around the playground, an utter wreck.

L. Record the following sentence on the white board:
Valiantly, the Super Hero blasted rubble and glass to release the wailing teachers, even though the errant children begged him not to.
Read together.

M. Groups on A3 with felt tips; how many words the same or similar to 'valiantly' can you think up? Blu-Tack on windows. Walk along and read all. Choose the 2 words you like best. E.g. bravely / boldly / courageously / heroically.

N. Thesaurus Game, look up the synonyms for 'valiant' while teacher counts back from 10 to 0.

O. Pairs; discuss what you think 'errant' means in that sentence. Explain why they think that.

P. Dictionary race, look up meaning of 'errant' while count back from 10 to 0.

Q. Make up a Power Sentence about 'the errant children'.

Cool Down

A. In pairs, group words for: cows / dogs / lions / geese / fish / whales = herd / pack/ pride / flock / shoal / school).

Next Time… repeat lesson with a different 'WOW' word = infinite lessons.

9. Athletic Up-Levelling Lesson

Objective 1: To widen children's vocabulary.
Objective 2: To raise standards in writing.

Requirements:
Personal whiteboards and felt tips.

 **Start Lesson Here**

A. What level are these two sentences and how do you know? Teacher records the 2 sentences on the white board: The boy ran down the road. The boy fell down. (Level 1)

B. How could you make them Level 2? Quickest way is to join them with a connective. Name the Level 2 connectives. (and / but / so / then). Discuss the repetition of 'the boy' when it is one sentence and agree to change second use into the pronoun 'he'. Use each connective in turn. How does the meaning of the new, longer sentence change as you change the connective? Discuss.

C. Choose one and show on whiteboard.

D. Read the new Level 2 sentence together. How many doing words (verbs) are there? Find and name (2 = 'ran' and 'fell') Take the first, 'ran'. Pairs = whiteboards and felt tips, list as many synonyms (same or similar meaning) as you can think of. E.g. ran = trotted / sprinted / galloped / jogged…

E. "Show me".

F. Choose the one you like best and swap for 'ran'. Read new sentence together. E.g. The boy sprinted down the road and he fell over.

G. Take the second verb or doing word = 'fell'. Repeat paired synonyms work as in 'C'. E.g. tumbled / tripped / stumbled?

H. Choose the one you like best and swap for 'fell'. Read the new sentence together. E.g. The boy sprinted down the road and he tumbled over.

I. What level is the sentence now? (L3). Now it needs a describing word, an adjective to describe a noun or thing or an adverb to describe a doing word or verb. On whiteboards: list all the words that could have a describing word. Eg boy / sprinted / road / tumbled

J. Choose 'boy' and list the describing words that would be good Eg athletic / young / frightened / petrified / lithe / tall / small etcetera. Choose one and scribe the new sentence on the whiteboard. Read together. E.g. The petrified boy sprinted down the road and he tumbled over.

K. What does 'lithe' mean? Dictionary Race (see Appendix 2) for 'lithe'.

L. Dictionary Race against count back from 10 to 1 to find 'petrified' in the dictionary.

M. Thesaurus Race to find as many synonyms for 'petrified' as you can. Make up a sentence each using the word 'petrified'. It must be about a monster.

N. Share. E.g. Swiftly, the petrified boy ran from the fearsome monster.

O. Take a second word from the sentence e.g. 'road' and repeat the finding of describing words E.g. winding / leafy / long / endless / narrow / busy / congested / deserted etcetera.

P. Choose one and scribe the new sentence on the whiteboard. Read together. The petrified boy sprinted down the deserted road and he tumbled over.

Q. Are 'petrified' and 'deserted' adjectives or adverbs? (adjectives) Choose the verb or doing word 'sprinted'. Pairs list as many describing words or adverbs for 'sprinted' as they can e.g. swiftly / lithely / rapidly / hastily / desperately etcetera.

R. Choose one and insert. Read the new sentence together. The petrified boy sprinted swiftly down the deserted road and he tumbled over. Does this feel like a Level 4 yet?

S. Take the connective 'and'. Children discuss whether there are higher level connectives that could be used there. Prompt to think of time and sequence connectives. (Before / until / then) Try each one in turn and discuss the change in meaning as the connective changes. Choose one to use.

T. Which word could become a Power Opener in that sentence? Name the 3 Power Openers (Connectives / 'ly' words / 'ing' words. Which is the connective in that sentence and could it be an opener? ('and' = usually no, however the 2 higher level ones can be.) Is there an 'ing' word (no) but 'sprinted' could be changed to 'sprinting' to open the sentence. It could also be the 'ly' word, 'swiftly'. Encourage children to experiment with different options.

U. Pairs choose a Power Opener and work out how the new sentence would read. Scribe on the board and all read together.
E.g.
Swiftly sprinting down the deserted road, the petrified boy tumbled over.
Or
Before he tumbled over, the petrified boy sprinted swiftly down the deserted road.
Are these now Level 5 sentences?

 Cool Down

A. What could the boy be running from? Make up an 'ing' sentence to describe the cause of his fear.

Next Time…repeat the lesson with 2 different Level 1 sentences and a new focus = infinite lessons.

10. Ferdinand, My Imaginary Friend Lesson

Objective 1: To widen children's vocabulary.
Objective 2: To raise standards in writing.

Requirements:
A3 paper and felt tips.
Personal whiteboards.

 **Start Lesson Here**

A. "I have a new, imaginary friend today. He is called Ferdinand. How many alliterative (start with the same letter) words can you find for 'Ferdinand'?" Share and record on the white board. Eg friendly / furious / frightened / fearsome / foolish.

B. What sort of words are all these? (Describing words / adjectives)

C. Which alliterative word would we choose to make up an extension for Ferdinand's name? Eg Funny Ferdinand? Fast Ferdinand? Fruity Ferdinand? Fiery Ferdinand? Frantic Ferdinand? Friendly Ferdinand? Furious Ferdinand? Frightened Ferdinand? Fearsome Ferdinand? Foolish Ferdinand?

D. How would the name describe the character? Let's chose one. ('Fiery Ferdinand' for the sake of illustration).

E. Let's make up a character for Fiery Ferdinand. On A3 or A1 with fat markers, group discussion, draw him. List more describing words that do not have to be alliterative. Blu-tack along windows. Walk along and discuss the other groups' ideas. Are there words you would have liked to steal? How many 'WOW' words are there on each?

F. How many new words can you make up from the name 'Fiery Ferdinand' starting with 'f'? List as a group (A3 or white boards)

G. Show me. Record on white board. Discuss any doubtful ones or subtle ones. Eg Fred, fed, fad, fire, fine, fife, fare, fade, fan, far, fry, etcetera. Repeat the same activity starting the words with 'd'? Eg din, dead, dine, death. Repeat the same activity starting the words with 'r'? Eg red, ride rain, rare.

H. Teacher says; "Oh my goodness, Ferdinand did some writing in Big Writing last week. Just look at this. What has he forgotten to do?"

i have started in a new school i am in class X and it has lots of nice children in it yesterday we did art and i made a clay pot today we shall be going swimming tonight i am going to mc donalds with my mum and dad

I. We need to model how to punctuate this for Ferdinand. We shall read it together, naming all the changes and drawing them large in the air with our writing finger. I will show you how it will start.

"Capital 'I' have started in a new school full stop. Capital 'I' am in class X and it has lots of nice children in it full stop. Capital 'Y' Yesterday..."

Now, read it through in your head to work out where the changes go. Now talk about it in your group to see if you agree where the changes go.

Now, all together, saying and drawing (big in the air with your pointing finger) 1, 2, 3:

"Capital 'I' have started in a new school full stop. Capital 'I' am in class X and it has lots of nice children in it full stop. Capital 'Y' Yesterday we did art and capital 'I' made a clay pot full stop. Capital 'T' Today we shall be going swimming full stop. Capital 'T' Tonight capital 'I' am going to capital 'M' Mc capital 'D' Donald apostrophe 's' with my mum and dad full stop."

(This is best done with the children standing.)

J. Teacher says; "Well done everybody. Let's make the changes on the whiteboard. Shout each change for me as I make them". (Could be a click and drag activity).

Cool Down

Teacher says; "Cool down time everyone. Make up 3 alliterative sentences about Fiery Ferdinand; one about his favourite hobby, one about his favourite subject at school and one about his favourite food". For example, I could say,

"Fiery Ferdinand favours fast cars and flying in fantastic, fun filled flying machines".

"Do this as fast as you can, we are going to do each in turn against the clock. First, his favourite hobby or sport:

10; 9; 8; 7; etcetera or use a tambourine or similar. Make it fast, loud and lively. The count can be as slow or as fast as class can cope with.

Now his favourite subject at school: 10; 9; 8; etcetera

Now his favourite food: 10; 9; 8;

Well done and finish."

Additional Optional Activity:
Put up corrected passage from Ferdinand and use to up-level texts.

> **Next Time...** repeat with new samples of writing from new imaginary friends with new names focussing on a different initial letter = infinite lessons.

23

11. PE In The Hall Lesson

Objective 1: To widen children's vocabulary.
Objective 2: To raise standards in writing.

Requirements:
Copy of the poem on the whiteboard.
A3 paper and felt tips.

From 'The Little Book of Teacher Poems' by Ros Wilson

P.E. In The Hall
Big ball, little balls,
Stacks of cones in groups,
Bats and sticks and rackets
And multi-coloured hoops.
Boxes and benches
And ladders up the wall,
Our teacher works a miracle
To make a gym out of our hall.

 **Start Lesson Here**

- **A.** Read the poem twice with the class. Talk about the importance of reading with expression.
- **B.** In 2s: List as many synonyms for 'big' as you can (A3 & fat felt tips). Display with Blu-Tack on windows. (Eg large / huge / grand / massive / enormous. Discuss the subtle differences in meaning).
- **C.** Pairs move down line and 'steal' any they missed. Take their sheets down and add new ones to their lists. Relist in order of 'WOW' ness from least exciting to most. Could be a 'diamond ranking'. (E.g. 'huge', 'massive', 'enormous', 'gigantic, 'gargantuan', 'mountainous').
- **D.** Each choose 'favourite' of 'WOW' words for 'big'. Make up a sentence about our school using the word. Make up a sentence about our town / city / village using the word. Make up a sentence about Planet Earth using the word.
- **E.** Repeat 'B', 'C' and 'D' for the word 'little' (Use or do not use to adjust timings).
- **F.** In 2s: write a full sentence that incorporates the information in the first 4 lines of the poem. Find 3 places to insert an adjective (Eg there are big balls and little balls, groups of cones, bats, sticks, rackets and multi-coloured hoops). Make at least one of the adjectives a 'WOW' word. (E.g. "There are huge, blue balls and much smaller yellow balls stacked by the luminescent purple cones, an assortment of bats, sticks and rackets and the dazzling, multi-coloured hoops all laid out ready for today's P.E. lesson.")
- **G.** Change the structure of the sentence to provide a Power Opener: (E.g. "When we do P.E. there are..." or "During P.E. there are...").
- **H.** In 2s: Can you find a metaphor in the poem? Does the teacher really work a miracle? Why does the writer use that phrase? Can you name a 'miracle' your teacher works in the week?
- **I.** In 2s. Learn the poem. Recite together. Whole class recite. (This poem is easy to learn, by repeating 3 times, 2 or 4 lines at a time.)

J. Stand and work out movements to accompany the poem. Eg Big arm stretch for 'Big balls' / small, cupped hands for 'little balls / steepled arms for cones, repeated in a stacking pattern, moving upwards.

K. Perform the poem twice more with movements.

Cool Down

A. Class brainstorm of synonyms for 'stacks' Make me up... (E.g. 'piles', 'mounds', 'heaps', 'mountains of', etcetera).

Additional Optional Activity:
Follow up could be handwriting sheets (photocopied A4 plain with black felt inch border ruled). Write a copy of the poem in best handwriting and illustrate or decorate the border for the wall. It could be extended by up-levelling Ferdinand's paragraph.

> **Next Time...** Use other poems from 'The Little Book of Teacher Poems' by Ros Wilson to make up lesson = 40 LESSONS.

12. The Dinosaur Adventure Lesson

Objective 1: To widen children's vocabulary.
Objective 2: To raise standards in writing.

Requirements:
Copy of story (below) on the whiteboard or hard copy between 2.
Dictionaries. Mini whiteboards or A3 scrap paper. Felt tip pens. Blu-Tack.

From 'The Little PALS for Big Texts: Narrative' by Ros Wilson

"Hannah sat at her bedroom window, gazing forlornly over the newly mown lawn to the orchard beyond. It was the school holiday and all her friends were away, so Hannah was lonely and bored as she nibbled slowly at her honey sandwich. What could she do?

Suddenly, Hannah caught a glimpse of something moving through the blossoming fruit trees. At first she thought it was Chesney, one of her dogs, but she soon realised it wasn't. Hannah gasped in amazement... it was a very small dinosaur!

Hastily, Hannah sped down the stairs and out of the house. She crept stealthily across the lawn and concealed herself behind the huge holly bush. From her hiding place she watched the little dinosaur as it grazed peacefully in the shadows of the trees. It was about four feet high, with a spiny mantle down its back and a long, heavy tail. Its skin was rough, wrinkled and quite a startling green colour, and it had huge round eyes that shone like golden orbs."

 **Start Lesson Here**

- **A.** Read the passage as a class and in groups (if necessary, so that everyone can read it). Each group member chooses a 'WOW' word to 'steal'. Class brainstorm / record all WOW words on whiteboard with a score of how many times each had been chosen. Eg gazing / forlornly / nibbled / glimpse / gasped / amazement / hastily / sped / stealthily / concealed / grazed / mantle / startling / orbs.

- **B.** In 2s: Take a 'WOW' word in turn (from the whiteboard) and ask their partner what it means. If they know they score (on mini whiteboards or scrap paper). If they don't know and the asker does, he / she scores one instead. Keep a note of any words neither knows the meaning of. Check in dictionaries if unsure as to correctness.

- **C.** Show hands for which of the pair won. Whole class feedback to the teacher on meanings of the words.

- **D.** Dictionary Race (see Appendix 2) for any words no-one knew, if necessary.

- **E.** 'Make me up...' make up sentences with some or all of (depending on time) the 'WOW' words on the whiteboard, in pairs. The focus could be meeting a dinosaur OR finding something else unexpected in your garden.

- **F.** Now give down-levelled version below AND the high level above, printed on A4, to each pair.

From 'The Little PALS for Big Texts: Narrative' by Ros Wilson.

The Dinosaur Adventure

"Hannah sat at her bedroom window and looked out at the trees in the orchard. She was bored because it was a school holiday and all her friends had gone away. What could she do? Hannah slowly ate her honey sandwich.

Suddenly, Hannah saw something moving through the fruit trees. At first she thought it was one of her dogs, but then she realised it wasn't. It was a small dinosaur!

Hannah ran downstairs and out of the house. She crossed the lawn and hid behind the holly bush. From here she could see the little dinosaur. It was about four feet high with spines down its back. Its skin was rough and green, and it had round, orange eyes."

G. In pairs underline the lower word/s on the down-levelled text and use highlighters to highlight key up-levelling. Pink = 'WOW' word, blue = Power Openers, green = other good openers, yellow = Power Punctuation.

H. Teacher shows both passages together on whiteboard and takes feedback, underlining and highlighting. Pairs check against own.

I. Teacher fires Power Openers (not just from the passage) at pairs who make up a sentence against a count from 10 back to one, that opens with the Power Opener and is about an imaginary dinosaur. ('Suddenly...' 'Hastily...''Fortunately...' Furiously....''Unfortunately...''Roaring...' 'Thundering...' 'Towering...' 'Struggling...').

J. In pairs or threes, children list on A3 with bold felt tips, as many describing words and phrases as they can that might apply to a dinosaur's appearance. Move to share with another set and steal.

K. Children move round the room like dinosaurs. How do they feel? Add making a noise a dinosaur might make while moving round. How do they sound?

L. Repeat J with describing words for how he moves and again for how he sounds.

M. In pairs or threes, on A3, children make up and scribe a Power Sentence (2 Power Features) with description about a dinosaur. Could this be the next sentence of the story? Display with Blu-Tack on windows or wall. Walk along and read each other's.

 Cool Down

A. As teacher counts back from 10 to one, pairs / threes list as many antonyms to the initial 'WOW' words as able, on small whiteboards.

NB, for younger children, the first paragraph only might be used, at teacher's discretion.

Next Time… repeat with texts from the appendices = 10 lessons

Appendix 1: Pairs Of Text For 'Spot The Difference'

These texts are presented in pairs. The first version is mainly Level 3 / 4 threshold. Normally, if they were written by children, they would have a few errors in Basic Skills, which would push them down into Level 3. The second paragraph is usually Level 4 / 5 threshold. Normally it would need to be longer with a wider range of high level features to make it a secure Level 5.

It is recommended that children use the pairs of paragraphs to play 'Spot the Difference' by using three colours of highlighters to identify 'Power Features' in the higher level passage.

Power Features:
1. Power Words or WOW words.
2. Power Openers ('ly', 'ing' and connectives).
3. Power Punctuation = !, ?, ..., - OR one example of each sort of punctuation the writer has used.

The texts may then be used as the core of an adapted lesson to lesson 2 'Spot the Difference'.

These texts are also suitable for the class to continue and complete them in the up-levelled form, at a later date.

1. Victor Von Cleef

Victor Von Cleef is a punctuation thief. He goes into people's homes at night and he steals the punctuation from all their books. This makes it hard to read the stories so a lot of people are throwing their books away. This is very sad. Soon nobody will be reading books any more.

Victor Von Cleef, the punctuation thief, sneaks into people's abodes in the depths of the night and surreptitiously steals all the punctuation from every book. Reading a book is rendered extremely difficult through this evil practice and, as a result, many people are discarding their beloved texts. This is a tragedy! Possibly, it could lead to no-one ever enjoying books in the future.

2. Midnight Crash

The family slept in their beds. A loud crash woke them up. What could have happened? Father got up and put on his slippers and his dressing gown. He crept out onto the landing. He crept towards the stairs. A bit of plaster fell on his head. He looked up. What had crashed through the roof?

Soundly, the family slept in their cosy beds. All at once, a thunderous crash awakened them all. What disaster could have occurred? Bravely, the father leapt out of bed and donned his dressing gown and slippers. Surreptitiously, he crept out onto the shadowy landing and edged stealthily towards the stairs. To his horror a fragment of plaster struck him on the head. Father peered upwards... "My goodness," he gasped in horror, "What on earth has smashed through our roof?"

3. The Race

The children talked and laughed as they lined up for the last race. The teacher held up the starting gun and they all went quiet. The gun fired and the children started running down the track. Shona really wanted to win. She tried really hard. She passed one child after another. There was only one more child to pass. Shona gave one last try.

Chattering and laughing cheerfully, the children lined up for the start of the final race. Silence fell as the teacher raised the starting gun. The gun fired! Swiftly the children sprinted down the track. Desperate to win, Shona gave her very best. She powered past child after child until, at last, there was only one more opponent to overtake. Drawing a huge breath, Shona threw herself forward in one final surge. Could she make it?

4. Night in the Playroom.

It was quiet in the playroom. The children were asleep in bed. Toys lay around on furniture and on the floor. They were lying where the children had left them. A moon beam appeared round the corner of the curtain and lit the room. Teddy opened his eyes and stretched his tired old arms and legs. He stood up carefully on his shelf and he climbed down, onto the dolls' house roof then down onto the big Tonka truck and onto the floor. He looked round at all the toys. Who should he wake up?

Hushed and silent, the playroom was still as the children were slumbering in another place. Discarded toys lay on the furniture and floor, just as the children had left them. Slowly, a dazzling moonbeam emerged round the corner of the curtain and lit up the darkness like a bright spot light. Cautiously, Teddy opened his eyes. Stretching his tired, old limbs and yawning gingerly, he rose to his feet on his narrow shelf and quietly but carefully he climbed down.... first onto the roof of the dolls' house, then onto the cab of the mighty Tonka truck. At last, safely, he stepped down onto the floor and gazed thoughtfully round at all the sleeping toys. Who should he wake up tonight?

5. The Puppy

The puppy looked at him. His brown eyes were sad. Jay wanted to buy him, but he did not have enough money. He walked home sadly. The next day was his birthday. His mother had put a big parcel by the breakfast table, all wrapped in blue paper. Jay opened it quickly. Inside was the puppy. Jay was so happy.

The adorable puppy gazed at Jay with huge, brown eyes. Jay desperately wanted to purchase him, but he did not have sufficient money. Sadly, he walked home. The following day was his birthday. Jay came down stairs to find his mother had placed a large parcel wrapped in shiny, blue paper beside the breakfast table. Swiftly opening the package, Jay found it contained the very same, adorable puppy. He was ecstatic!

6. A Day at the Sea

It seemed so long since Max and Ria had seen the sea. They were so excited as their father drove them the sixty miles to the coast. They sang songs and played 'I Spy' with their parents. At last they began the long drive down through Seaborough. They both stared ahead. They both hoped to be the first to see the sea. Then it was in front of them. They looked at the blue sea with smiles on their faces.

It seemed an age since Max and Ria had last seen the sea. As their father drove them the sixty miles across country to the coast, they were bubbling with excitement. To pass the time, they sang songs and played 'I Spy' with their parents. At last they commenced the long drive down through the sleepy town of Seaborough, both of them peering ahead in an effort to be the first to spy the sea. Suddenly, there it lay before them. Smiles spread over their faces as they gazed in awe at the sparking, azure ocean.

7. The Messenger.

The wind blew hard. It was wild. The trees bent over. Their branches looked like arms reaching out. Lyall walked into the wind. It was a struggle. Rain hit his face. He felt as though he was trying to break through a big wall. Sometimes he thought of turning back and going home. He could not, it was too important. He had to get the message across the boundary.

Howling and screaming, the wild wind buffeted the countryside. Trees bent before it in submission, their branches stretched forward like arms, appealing for respite. Head down, Lyall staggered into the ferocious gale. It was a struggle! Icy rain battered into his face, blinding him. Pushing ever forward, Lyall felt as though he was attempting to smash through an impenetrable wall. At times he contemplated turning back... returning home. However, he could not, for it was too important. It was imperative that he got this crucial message across the border.

8. The Island

They saw the island first as the sun rose over the horizon. It rose slowly from the calm sea. It looked small. It was all green and its coastline was white beaches. The small, battered boat sailed forward. The twins tried hard to keep it on course. Its torn sails flapped uselessly and the small, emergency engine coughed at the faster speed. The island came nearer. They would be safe.

Dawn broke over the calm, ocean as the twins first spotted the island. Slowly, it rose from the turquoise waters. At a distance, it appeared small, densely covered with foliage of many greens and with silver, coral sands fringing its coast. The small, battered boat surged forward. Desperately, the twins fought to keep the weary vessel on course. Torn sails flapped ineffectively whilst the tiny emergency engine spluttered in protest at the increased speed. Slowly the island drew nearer.... at last they would be safe!

9. The Missing Boy.

"Where is he?" Mrs. Hyatt looked down the road. She had thought her small son was still playing in the garden, but when she came out to check the gate was open and Joe was not there. Mrs. Hyatt was scared. Had he gone off down the road? She did not know how long he had been gone. She ran down the road as fast as she could.

"Where is he?" Desperately, Mrs. Hyatt peered along the busy road. Assuming that her young son was still playing safely in the garden, she was horrified to come outside and find the gate ajar and... her son not there! Could he have wandered away down the road? Not knowing how long he had been missing, she raced down the congested thoroughfare as swiftly as she could.

10. The Fairy Queen

The fairies sat in silence on their toadstools. The elves were in one group at the side, whispering to each other. They knew they were going to hear something important. The queen of the fairies did not call them together very often. What could it be? Then they heard the noise of horses trotting down the lane. A gold carriage came round the corner, pulled by four white horses. In the back of the carriage sat their queen. She was tall and proud with her shiny crown and sparkling wings.

Silence fell over the glade as the anxious fairies settled on the luminous surfaces of their toadstool seats. To one side gathered the whispering elves, all huddled in one snuggle together. Something important was to happen, for the Queen of the Fairies rarely called them all together in this way.

What could it be? At last they heard the clattering of horses' hooves on the gravelly lane and a golden carriage appeared round the bend, drawn by four white stallions. Sitting in the rear of the carriage, tall and proud, was their Queen, resplendent in her sparkling, gold crown and magnificent gossamer wings.

11. First Train Ride

Foz couldn't believe it. He was on a train. He was twelve years old and he had never been on a train before. He had been on cross Channel ferries and even on a cruise ship. He had been on the biggest 'planes and even in a hot air balloon, but he had not been on a train. Foz gazed out of the window at the countryside rushing by. He loved the speed and the noise of the wheels on the tracks. They were going over 120 miles an hour. It was great.

He couldn't believe it…he was on a train. Foz was twelve years old, yet he had never experienced travel by train before. He had been on massive cross channel ferries, ploughing through the turbulence of the English Chanel and even on a mighty cruise ship once. He had flown in huge passenger aeroplanes and even in a hot air balloon, but never had he experienced the wonder of this train journey. Foz gazed out of the window as the countryside raced past. He loved the phenomenal sensation of speed and the rhythm of the wheels clacking on tracks. They were hurtling along at over 120 miles per hour. It was amazing!

12. Night Visitors

The people of Ganda slept well in their beds. The only thing moving was the owl's eyes. He sat on the barn roof and watched for the mice. The air was still and the sky was black except for the stars. There was a noise and a very bright light raced across the sky. It fell over the horizon. No-one saw it drop into the deep woods. A puff of smoke rose up through the trees and a noise made the ground shake. It sounded as if a door was swinging open.

The people of Ganda slumbered soundly in their beds. The night was still and silent, nothing moved save for the slow blink of the wise owl's eye. Perched on the roof of the barn, he watched, patiently, for the mice that he knew would eventually pass his way. Still air and inky black sky, pierced only by the twinkling of stars, enveloped the sleeping town. Suddenly a soft 'whoosh' shattered the silence as a dazzlingly bright light pierced the darkness and streaked across the sky. No-one observed as it plunged over the horizon and disappeared into the depths of the dark woods. Through the canopy of the trees there rose a fine plume of smoke, as a low, grinding noise made the very earth vibrate… as if a huge door was slowly swinging open.

Appendix 2: Activity Glossary

1. Call My Bluff:

- **A.** Teacher puts an unknown (to children) WOW word on the board, followed by 3 definitions, only one of which is right.
  E.g. Copious = 1. A group of trees   2.   A lot of things   3. A warm cloak
- **B.** The children (in 2s or 3s) read the word and discuss each definition in turn.
- **C.** They 'guess' which may be the right meaning.
- **D.** They record A, B or C on their whiteboards or scrap paper.
- **E.** They hold them up when the teacher asks them to. (If time, they may walk round and show their answer to other groups and discuss why they thought that before being asked to show them).
- **F.** If time is short, the teacher gives the right answer.
- **G.** If there is time, there is a Dictionary Race to find the right meaning.

2. Dictionary Race:

- **A.** The teacher writes a target WOW word (unknown to the children as yet) on the board.
- **B.** While the teacher counts back from 10 to 1, or uses a timer, the children 'race' to find the correct definition in dictionaries.
- **C.** If time, they then make up sentences using the word. If no time, this should be done in 'Bells Work'.

3. Thesaurus Race:

- **A.** The teacher writes a target WOW word (unknown to the children as yet) on the board.
- **B.** While the teacher counts back from 10 to 1, or uses a timer, the children 'race' to find three or more similes in thesauruses.
- **C.** This may be played as an extension to the same word as in the Dictionary Race.
- **D.** The 'game' continues as in the Dictionary Race.

4. Bells Work:

The teacher uses the few minutes at the ends of lessons and sessions
(or waiting for shared space to be free) to ask children to make up sentences using new WOW words they are learning.

5. The 3 Power features:

- **A.** Ambitious Vocabulary = WOW Words or Power Words
- **B.** Power Openers (see below)
- **C.** Power Punctuation (see below)

6. Power Openers:

A. Open a sentence with a connective eg 'Before...' 'After...' 'Because...' 'Despite...' 'Instead of...'

B. Open a sentence with an 'ly' word (adverb) eg 'Slowly...' 'Rapidly...' 'Thoughtfully...'

C. Open a sentence with an 'ing' word (participle) eg 'Walking...' 'Hoping...' 'Remembering...' 'Fearing...'

7. Power Punctuation:

A. Use of any of the 3 'easy to use but have quick impact' pieces of punctuation = ? (question mark), ! (exclamation mark), ... (ellipses).

B. Use of any of the harder but powerful pieces of punctuation = all Level 5.

Appendix 3: Hyperlink To Bank Of Interesting Images

www.andrelleducation.co.uk/LessonPlansImages/Images.zip

1. Type the hyperlink into the address bar of your internet browser and press enter.
2. When presented with download options click 'Save'.
3. Unzip the folder of images for use in lessons where appropriate.